Ocean of Hearts

Muhsina Kealamthodi

 pencil

ISBN 978-93-5667-201-7
© Muhsina Kealamthodi 2022
Published in India 2022 by Pencil

A brand of
One Point Six Technologies Pvt. Ltd.
123, Building J2, Shram Seva Premises,
Wadala Truck Terminal, Wadala (E)
Mumbai 400037, Maharashtra, INDIA
E connect@thepencilapp.com
W www.thepencilapp.com

DISCLAIMER: *The opinions expressed in this book are those of the authors and do not purport to reflect the views of the Publisher.*

Author biography

Muhsina Kealamthodi from Kerala she love to travel with time' love to write poems and stories novel etc..

CONTENTS

Butterfly Heart

Only one Moon

Only one ocean

You under earth wakeup me

Glass of mirror made soul

Unimaginable Little Fantasy

rarely meet in the world

I see you ten thousand years

before ago You walk into the my heart

Butterfly heart in made beautifully designed

Every colour of the heaven

Fuel heart in you both destiny of butterfly Eye

' learn the art of heart

Click here to visit story'

songIt's a magic butterfly heart

Only wonder window Sensory of Wonderful

butterfly Sky only white snow

You come colour rainbow magicA butterfly heart

Ocean Heart'

Blue light of the heaven

Night moon white snow

Dazzling my whole heart

Be my light

Come with angel eyes

Complete ocean with you

Incomplete without you

Raining all day's in the underlying

Ocean wild fairy tale glass of magic'

Ocean up and down

Running eagerly towards you

It's beautiful Longley tried heart'

Made in the world

Mysterious sound of your heart

Touching sleepless night

Ocean of Hearts

Classy and elegant design you
Bright blue diamond Moonlight
Shining unconditional love
Surprising how to love you

Mind is unimaginable happiness
Unbelievable beauty uniquely
You thrilling fantasy world
Longley Moon

Nature wind cloud ocean
Seen blue ocean
In your eyes
Little Fantasy
Ocean heart'..

Diamond Heart

Diamond stone my inner soul
Heart touching still alive
Visual changing the way
Dreaming of different imagination

Coding for windows light
Sky where belong
Seem look strange to me
Draining the sky
Diamond Moon Face to Face
Running wondering you are the most
Beautiful soul

Laying on a million times
Over the wall
Keep your smile on my way

SoulFul Heart

Travel time from in my heart
Soul that belong to me
Bury billion years
Begin again

Conquer what belong to me
Sense of control
Already in mine

Corridor corpus of your heart
A wonderful soul
I dreaw a line toward your heart
You welcome to me

I passing through the centuries of circle
I only remember you
Because you are me

Purple Heart

You coloured my world
With Fully love enternal beauty
I reborn as a blue violet flower

Purple Heart of the sky
Need for you
Dreaming of you
mightbe able to see you again

Like my heart day and night
I really want to a purple flower smile
conquerthe your heart

Garden angle of the heaven
Come to me
Found my eyes only drop shadow your heart
But you color with your heart
Designed to be a heaven

Magic Heart

Draining your eyes magintic love

Inculcate you are my angel

Butterfly heart in glass bridge crossing my soul

Touching my robotic heart

Made in misrable life

But you knock the door

I am open my heart for you

You are fantastic fantasy world

I want you only look at the mirror eyes

For me because

It's galaxy of pourity

Pouring rain happiness

Incomplete disert chilly cool

Warm your soul

Unique Heart

Beautiful memories of love

A long time ago mountain view

Very peace in the earth

Walking in the sky

See a mirror of moon

cometo the same time

Light up moon

So try to build kingdom

For her remember me

capture her soul that belong to me

Destiny Call you

Come back home

A unique Heart

romanceand me

Red Rose Heart'

Fragrance of you my soul in peace
I love the feeling come to me
Going find the truth
Fragrance of you
Come to me the night

Night so long but it was more worstful
I can't find anything
Be the best most beautiful red rose gold smile
on your face on you

Red Rose valley of the heaven
See you that magintic love
Remember fragrance never forget you
My all' the life
Soul kind of purity of heart

Enternal Heart'

You believe me when I can't believe

Enternity of my heart

You show me magic' fantasy

Beating without heart'

Stone collect build heaven

For you

Shall I send it desplay

Call miracle in Rainbow

Find beauty leave a dandelion root

Imagination creative smile

There is more darkness reach shining

Enternal Fragrance of bright own soul

I thought you would be lovely

But you are angle

Come from heaven..

Mirror Heart'

Mirror Soul' selves to kindly book
Bright glass of water
Fallen into the Star in the world
Only glass mirror is magic

For you only touch my heart
That's mirror of moon
Only the full moon

When the time passing through my heart
Flaying high there is a sky
Make a beautiful flower magic'
Mirror Soul' selves my eyes

Begin to end that is my new way
Top gallery heart'
Only made mirror

Moon Heart'

Darkness of night open the door

A moon smile

Billion years after find you

My moon fantasy heart'

Calm the time to explore new beginning

Dancing in the sky

Moon early morning

All' around the shine star

written already in your name

There only one Moon

Everything is going to your moon

Shallow depth of field of mine

Always remember your heart'

Vanlia Heart

Vanlia sweet little bit wait
Until magic chocolate drink
Coffe teasty smell fantasy world
Deeply down to the sweetest heart'

Dream only show favorite sweetness of you
Magnetic soul fragrance Flame alive
Unknown tonnes of my whole heart
Try to build Vanlia fantasy
Fully ocean sky rainbow magic
Wonder

Touching sleepless nights
Brought to creamy white snow
Orange
Holly springs water falls ocean
Only teast sweet smile
Rotating the sky

Blue Heart

Blue cross shield of faith
Million times in your breath
Count on me magic'
Blue heart'

Build your heart towards my favourite
Faith in the blue flowers
You believe me
When darkness come teast sweetheart
Blomed happy colour
My blue heart'

Missing way' bleeding calm
Feeling every time low high
Remember the memory
whispering rain night
All' see you

Blooming Heart'

Magnetic field of mine
Blooming fragrance smell
Flooding in the sky
Dreaming of different imagination

Calling bell lost centuries
Time moving never be mine
Ever since I found you
Magnetic field of the sky

Where is the place
Where is the time
Where are you ?
Blooming Heart' only one

Come in the jelly belly field
Fold the time most convenient
Place mountains tope
Look at the mirror
Blooming my heart

Fragrance Heart'

My heart Fragrance of your heart
Wetherless leaving the intended solely
Cartoon of a beautiful Iceland
Last updated on smiling face
walkingin the door

How to love you
Fragrance Flame alive in my dead ghost
Sleeping in the earth nothing compared to
Aliveness but beatles count machine
Slowly growing direction
Where you Fragrance soul

Till the end begin
time again for your smile
Magic lamp fantased you
Still there is a sky
You Fragrance my heart
Over my pain'

Light Heart'

Lighting up deadless heart
Only more beautiful memories
December fantastic thanks
Magic of weather

Every morning view much better today
I was I will morning in the earth
Just like you
Very nice fantasy

Hoping to hear from heart made glass
bridge clear pure everything
In there is a great gift
Rose could be a heaven on earth
It's a magic shooting for me

Heaven Heart'

Me meaning of you
Silencely see you again
A heaven Heart'

Rotating the summer Vibes
let me believe in you
So find me in your heart

A beautiful flower
Only come to me
A beautiful winter time
Only you warm love

Miles travel with you
Are you ready to hold special you
With me
A summer Vibes

Winter Heart'

Winter in you are not realize something coming
My heart winter boil with smile on your face
It's worth living in time

White snow cover my soul
Cold weather make fall
Warmness you come to me
Like wind Flowing fast
Touching sleepless nights
Knowing that is the best medicine your heart
Everywhere you follow me
When longlines down
Everything in me
You keep warm..
Your heart

Angel Heart

Angel in my life

Take my hand forever with you

I don't want go anywhere

Where you I want there

Please tell me

Come fast not despair suddenly

Lovely dream Longley tried heart'

Show more beautiful ways love you

I keep getting our own soul happiness

Found heaven soul

I in you Fragrance soul you belong to me

Heart

Heart sprinkles waves of unspoken words
Solve the thousand years passed away
Time to explore new beginning
Heart touching still alive

Heart will find you
That' destiny of her
I own your love
Enjoy your infinity love
Come from heaven

Infinity Heart

Holly willing to do infinity scarf
Surround sound like calling me
Holding a sign that says you are my angel
It's true infinity heaven
Backing my heart
Saying you are my angel

Delicious destiny you come
Evaluation of the sky
Found in the door your eyes
Open it for me

Updated on smiling face walking through
In shadow of the smell
When you come here
Infinity Heart of my heart

Legend heart'

Valuable inside presious outside
You are legend

More you are mind-blowing
Waiting for you

Know your heart let in me
Your eyes

In my life there is legend
It is you

Courisity Heart'

Be it's been mysterious light
Founded in thousand years ago
More familiar name
Come in the wind

Fallen into y fairy dream
Connect on magic of time
Like more courisity Heart'

Fantasy Heart

Who is the fantasy world
Who made distance to the fantasy
Record all' the sound

I am living Fantasy drew
Long time vision very nice
Remember me

Silver Heart

On the radio romance between two soul

Find all true

Calm the time to explore

newbeginning of the heaven

Every one of the smile

Drewing to your home

Caching breathing air

Rewrite silver Heart

Strawberry Heart'

Strawberry Love blue diamond

Moonlight night

Half of the moon

Look at you remember me

Complete me

Streaming with her smiler my heart

Drowning in the eyes

Only in my strawberry Heart'

Rainbow Heart'

Rain falling endlessly

Peaceful rainbow Skech

Write a letter

It's easy to get

But high' to touch

Colourful history of the heaven

It is rainbow magic